This book is to be returned on or before
the last date stamped below.

THOMAS TELFORD SCHOOL
TELFORD SHROPSHIRE

FEED THE
BIRDS

FEED THE
B·I·R·D·S

Tony Soper

Illustrated by Kevin Baker

DAVID & CHARLES

Page 2 Blue tit in a nest box *(B. Borrell/FLPA)*

British Library Cataloguing in Publication Data
Soper, Tony
  Feed the birds
  1. Great Britain. Birds. Observation
  I. Title
  598.0723441

  ISBN 0–7153–9464–9

Typeset by ABM Typographics Ltd Hull
and printed in Singapore
by Saik Wah Press
for David & Charles plc
Brunel House   Newton Abbot   Devon

Contents

1   First become a Birdwatcher   6

2   Feed the Birds   14

3   Birds need Water as well   35

4   Somewhere to Nest   47

5   Bird Table Watching   73

6   A Career with Birds   87

Useful Addresses   92

Further Reading   93

Index   95

First become a Birdwatcher

Learn to use the tools of the trade . . .

BIRDWATCHING is a kind of hunting. But instead of killing the birds to fill our bellies, we are bagging them as trophies in our notebooks. To be successful at the job, we must use old-time hunters' tricks. Fieldcraft involves a great deal more than wearing a camouflaged jacket. The hunter must know his prey, above all he needs to know about time and place. Wildlife photographers also face the problems of the hunter, and the best ones are those to whom a knowledge of natural history comes first, before knowledge of cameras and lenses.

Putting a name to a bird is probably the first requirement in getting to know something about it. And a knowledge of bird topography is an important foundation in the building up of identification expertise. The editors of *British Birds* magazine have produced the comprehensive and authoritative 'British Standard' charts on page 8 in the hope that everyone will use the same language.

The tools of the trade are important. Keen eyesight and hearing are the naturalist's most precious assets. Observation by sight and sound is the basis of all fieldwork. Perhaps the observer's notebook and pencil come next, for the best memory in the world is no substitute for on-the-spot recording.

Binoculars are indispensable, but cause great heart-searching to many would-be birdwatchers. The problem is that, like birds, they come in a bewildering variety of forms. To face every situation you need half-a-dozen pairs. However, given that you are to start by buying one pair, you should go for glasses that are reasonably light in weight and which give a bright picture over a medium field of view, with a magnification of eight or nine times and objective

Great tits will always find holes in walls, especially if they lead to cavities big enough for a nest *(Eric & David Hosking)*

Chaffinch nests get full marks for neatness *(David Hosking)*

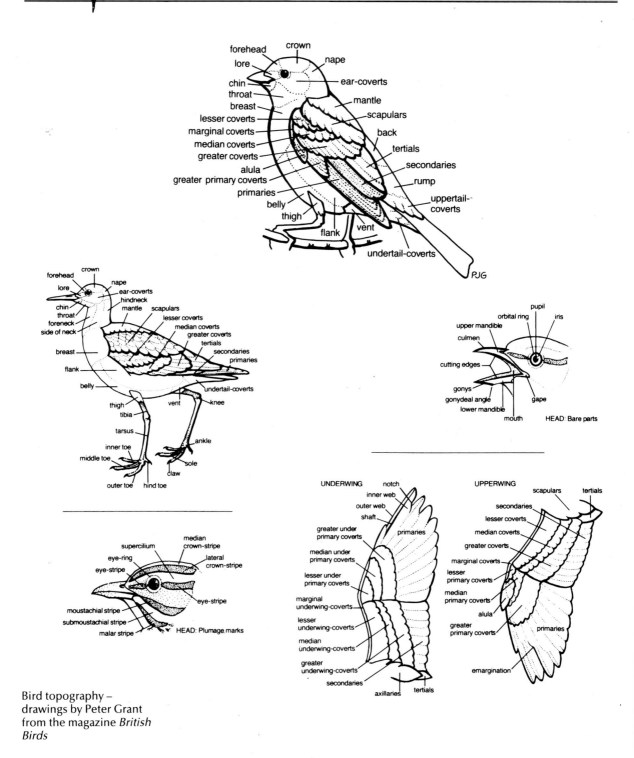

Bird topography –
drawings by Peter Grant
from the magazine *British Birds*

Estimated numbers of some familiar garden birds in the British Isles, mid-winter. (Figures taken from BTO *Atlas of Wintering Birds in Britain and Ireland.*)

Wren	12–20 million	Blue tit	15 million
Dunnock	20 „	Great tit	10 „
Robin	10 „	Nuthatch	60,000+
Blackbird	14–20 „	Magpie	750,000+
Song thrush	6–10 „	Starling	37 million
Redwing	1+ „	House sparrow	10–15 „
Goldcrest	2–4 „	Chaffinch	30 „
Blackcap	3000	Bullfinch	1 „

lenses between thirty and forty millimetres in diameter. Thus your chosen binoculars might be described as 8x30 or 9x40, both good for everyday work. Lower or higher magnifications should go hand in hand with higher light-gathering power, eg 7x50 or 10x50, the first being ideal for marine use, when you must reduce the problems of unwanted rock and roll on a moving boat, and the second about as powerful as most people can hold without getting a wobbly picture.

Avoid 'bins' with magnification greater than 10 until you are experienced enough to use them to advantage. Avoid zoom binoculars, which will be heavy and optically poor. And avoid anything that presents you with a blurred image anywhere in the picture or shows halo effects. Get the opinions of other birdwatchers and get hold of a field guide pamphlet called *Binoculars and telescopes* published by the British Trust for Ornithology, Beach Grove, Tring, Herts.

Focussing

Binoculars need focussing both for different distances and for different people's eyesight. The two eye-pieces are either focussed separately or together by a central milled wheel. Although separate focussing is stronger and more weatherproof, central focussing is much easier, needing only one finger to operate. Modern binoculars are all focussed by means of a central wheel, while some older binoculars have individual eye-piece focussing. Avoid 'instant-focus' bins, they are just a gimmick.

Range

Although all binoculars can be focussed on far-away objects, they vary greatly at short distances. Many birdwatchers have found that when trying to focus on a nearby bird they have to step back before it can comfortably be watched without eye strain. Regrettably, some of the more expensive binoculars fail in this respect. This can easily be overlooked when buying, but it is important for any close-up bird study. Someone with 'long sight' has to be particularly careful because, with a given pair of binoculars, he cannot focus as close as someone with normal or 'short sight'. Those who wear glasses

Robin at nest *(Roger Wilmshurst/FLPA)*

Blackbirds make a mud cup for a nest, lining it with grasses *(David Hosking)*

Worms come to the surface to feed at night, then hide away as the sun rises, so it *is* true that the early bird catches the worm *(Eric & David Hosking)*

Checking binoculars

(This is especially important if you're thinking of buying a second-hand pair.)

1   Check mechanically; make sure that the focussing wheel moves freely, that the cross-piece joining the eye-pieces is unwarped and fairly rigid; and that the body is sound.

2   Look through the binoculars the wrong way round (through the large lens) for flaws or deterioration of the lenses or dirt on their surfaces.

3   Check that the lenses are coated by looking at them (not *through* them); they should have a uniform blue, green or yellow tinge.

4   Look at some distant small object against the sky — the top of a television aerial or flag pole is ideal. Make sure that you can see only one image, without any eye strain.

5   Look at the television aerial again, see if it stays sharp as you swing the glasses sideways. There is a certain amount of blurring near the edges with all binoculars, but it should remain sharp for at least the centre half of the lens.

6   Make sure that the television aerial, when in the centre of the lens, does not appear to have a blue border on one side and an orange one on the other. This is important, otherwise the colours of birds will be distorted. As you swing the glasses again, coloured borders should not appear markedly in the centre half of the lens.

7   Look at any vertical line — a pole or side of a building. As you swing the binoculars sideways, the line will appear to bend, but this distortion should not happen near the centre of the lens.

8   Check for close range — see how close you can focus.

9   Focus on some detailed objects (such as a newspaper pinned up 20 yards — or 20 metres — away), see how sharp it is, and, if possible, compare with other binoculars.

10   Check for brightness of the image, comparing with other binoculars.

11   Consider their weight and remember that they may have to hang around your neck for many hours.

12   Are they comfortable to hold? This will help to determine how easy they will be to use.

can usually, if they have simple 'long' or 'short' sight without astigmatism, use binoculars without their glasses. But if you have to use your glasses, you will find that, because you cannot put the binoculars close to your eyes, the field of view is greatly restricted. Most new binoculars have turn-down rubber cups which help to a certain extent. A few of the more expensive makes can be custom-designed to accommodate special optics for spectacle wearers.

During the trial stage, it is probably best to enjoy the relatively cheap 'Avocet' glasses sold by the RSPB. Write to the Sales Dept, RSPB, The Lodge, Sandy, Bedfordshire for a copy of the Sales Catalogue. See what the people in your local RSPB or YOC group use. You'll learn a lot by borrowing their bins on your first outings. But when you've finally chosen the power which suits you, I'm afraid the best advice is to buy the most expensive you can afford.

Field Guides

There are several field guides to identification — hunters' manuals. Peterson, Mountford and Hollom's *Field Guide to the Birds of Britain and Europe* was first published by Collins in 1954 and has enjoyed high approval by birdwatchers ever since. The current edition is completely revised and up to date. Both Heinzel, Fitter and Parslow's *The Birds of Britain and Europe* and *The Hamlyn Guide to the Birds of Britain and Europe* by Bertel Bruun have the great advantage of a layout which combines text, maps and drawings so that they appear on the same page for each bird.

As for general introductions to bird biology and behaviour, there are excellent books by David Saunders (*RSPB Guide to British Birds*, published by Hamlyn, 1975), by Peter Conder (*RSPB Guide to Birdwatching*, published by Hamlyn, 1978), and by James Fisher and Jim Flegg (*Watching Birds*, T. & A.D. Poyser, 1974).

You will also need a more encyclopaedic volume of background information, species by species, and this is well catered for by P.A.D. Hollom in *The Popular Handbook of Rarer British Birds*, Witherby, 1980.

Books are notoriously useless at helping with the sounds made by birds. Yet calls and songs are often a vital clue to identification. The best way to learn the birdsong is by way of a knowledgeable companion, but a good gramophone record or tape will help. Jeffery Boswall has edited a set of recordings by Sture Palmer in 'A Field Guide to the Birdsongs of Britain and Europe', which is available (from the RSPB, for instance) in both disc and cassette form. John Kirby's 'Wildtrack' cassettes are also available from the RSPB.

Feed the Birds

LIKE US, birds need food, water and shelter. As fuel, food provides energy, promotes health, allows for defence capability and reproduction. Water is equally important, not just for drinking but for the maintenance of plumage. Lastly, shelter provides protection from enemies and the elements and serves as a nursery.

A mature garden with plenty of shrubs and flowering plants, with a mix of young, prime and decaying trees (some clad in ivy), an orchard with lichen-encrusted trees and surrounded by thick hedges, and containing a house with plenty of corners and ledges, is a good place for birds. The highest bird density in Britain is found in suburban gardens and estates, where the habitat resembles an endless woodland edge. Develop your garden for the maximum nut, berry, seed and insect production, to provide cover and water. In a newly-planted garden, which will inevitably lack abundant bird food, a bird table will be most important. But the long-term plan should be to provide as varied and plentiful a mix of natural food as possible.

Robins, thrushes, sparrows, starlings and dunnocks are all happy to live alongside us and will soon take advantage of new housing estates. On the other hand, many of our summer visitors, such as warblers, need a bit of encouragement so provide foliage and flowers which support a lot of insects.

A variety of 'weeds'

Try to keep a wilderness area in part of your garden, a wild jungle of weeds and shrubs that can be visited by hunting bands of finches. A clump of nettles will be a breeding ground for insects and spiders,

Peanuts are a great tit's best friend, but only if they are guaranteed safe from Aflatoxin; make sure you buy 'safe nuts'. *(Trevor Beer)*

and butterflies will lay their eggs on the leaves. If possible, the wilderness should have a dark and secret roosting-place where birds may rest and recuperate, but the most important factor is a flourishing variety of seed-producing 'weeds'.

Nettles are good value — and beautiful, too. Other suitable plants are thistles, knapweed, teazel, ragwort, groundsel, chickweed, dandelion and dock. The advantage of these native plants is that they offer first-class feeding to birds which are well equipped to exploit them. Goldfinches, for example, use their long probing bills to extract the seeds from prickly thistle and teazel heads. It is true that wild thistles run riot; the ornamental varieties, which are more restrained, still produce plenty of seeds. Cow parsley, that vigorous and glorious hedgerow edge plant, should be a welcome member of the wilderness community, and greenfinches much enjoy its seeds. And the same is true of fat hen, a plant disliked by 'real' gardeners but enjoyed by finches when they go for the seeds in late summer.

The best bird gardens offer a variety of habitat

Goldfinches have long bills so that they can probe into thistle heads for the seeds

Bramble should find a place somewhere. Apart from providing good roosting and nesting potential, its flowers support insects, comma caterpillars feed on its leaves and, in due course, thrushes and blackbirds take the berries.

Lawns and lawn-watching

An open and well-kept lawn is a priceless asset to the bird-rich garden. It provides a courting arena for pigeons, a battleground for blackbirds, and a great deal of choice food. Artificial and man-made though it may be, the green sward is a constant attraction to bug, beast and bird.

The old saying about the early bird getting the worm is an exact observation of fact. Worms are creatures of moisture and mildness, early morning dew suits them, whereas the warmth of sunrise causes them to return underground. So thrushes and blackbirds comb the lawn at first light, and this is when you may see the bigger blackbird steal worms from the song thrush, thus getting his breakfast the easy way.

Some of the lawn visitors are looking for grass and weed seeds, and of these perhaps the most attractive is the goldfinch. The sight

Sometimes a bit of careful pruning can make a space for a nest

left
This blue tit is sharing the
peanut feeder with a
siskin, a small finch that
has taken to invading
suburban gardens
(Brian Hawkes)

Goldfinches have beaks
that are specially adapted
to teasing out the seeds
from teazle heads
(A. R. Hamblin/FLPA)

of a 'charm' of goldfinches attacking the golden dandelions ought to be enough to convert any gardener into a dandelion fan. They approach them with zest, leapfrogging onto stems, landing about halfway up towards the head so that they weigh it down to the ground. Then they get to work. All finches are seedeaters, with powerful jaw muscles and bills modified for husking. They have two grooves inside the bill which locate the nut or seed, then the tongue rotates it as the mandibles crush. The husk peels off, leaving the kernel to be swallowed. Different finches go for different seeds; a hawfinch, for example, is tough enough to cope with cherry and plum stones, which take some cracking. Goldfinches, at the weaker end of the finch scale, use their relatively long, narrow bills rather as a pair of tweezers, probing deep into the seed head.

Swallows will occasionally settle on a lawn to pick from an ant swarm, but most of the time they are concerned with airborne flies. Perhaps the most spectacular lawn visitor (but one you're only likely to see if you live on the south coast) is the hoopoe. With its pinkish-brown plumage, barred black on the wings and back, it swoops onto the grass with a lazy flight. On landing, it shows a remarkable crest in the shape of a fan, pink with black tips. It struts about, probing into the soil with its long, decurved bill. Typically it prefers parkland, orchard and open-wooded country, but it is found near houses where it feeds on lawns and paths for insect larvae. A very few stay in Britain to nest, in holes or trees or buildings, and in some years there is quite an influx of them. One of the hoopoe's most endearing traits is its tameness and tolerance of man.

Ideally, trees in a garden should be of a mixed age, with young trees allowing plenty of light to reach the ground plants and prime trees providing an abundance of food and shelter. In the long run, decaying trees are the most valuable of all, allowing living space and providing sustenance to the greatest variety and number of insects and plants.

Fruit trees in an orchard supply lots of bird food, both in terms of insects and the fruit itself. Leave some of the fruit on a few of the trees so that it will decay gently into the kind of soft flesh for which thrushes are grateful in the winter. In summer, blue tits will hunt over apple trees and take quantities of the codling moth caterpillars which cause so much damage. Wild cherry is a good bird tree, but the sterile double-flowered cultivated varieties are of no value.

Hoopoe, with its crest
raised

Blackbirds and starlings, too, will be pleased to help you harvest
redcurrant and flowering currants. Of course, it is easy to object to
the way birds take their share of fruit and table vegetables, but on
the other side of the coin, starlings, for instance, eat large numbers
of leatherjackets.

Song thrushes enjoy
berries, straight from the
tree

Climbing plants

Trees, whether they are free-standing or part of a hedge system, may be much improved by teaming up with climbing plants. And if you cannot have trees at all, then at least erect some trellis or fencing to provide something for a climber like honeysuckle.

The much-maligned and ill-treated ivy should be treated with respect and cherished in any birdman's garden. It does no harm, except in the very rare cases when it completely covers the crown of a tree and so cuts off light to the foliage. It is also said that ivy sucks the goodness out of trees. This is untrue; ivy takes no nourishment, neither does it restrict the rate of growth of its 'host'. Ivy is a top-class birdman's plant. Thriving even in poor soil, it will carpet the ground till it finds an opportunity to climb. Climbing by virtue of the deceptively root-like hairs on its stem, ivy flowers when it reaches light. Flowering late, in September and October, it offers rich nectar at a time when this scarce commodity is particularly appreciated by butterflies, bees and other insects. Similarly, ivy fruits exceptionally late, in March and April of the next year, when its berries supply desperately needed food for wood pigeons and thrushes, to say nothing of a number of small mammals. Aside from this virtue, which should guarantee ivy a welcome in every garden, its evergreen secret places are a rich source of nest sites and roosting places. Throughout the year, its hairy stems and nourishing leaves support many insects, which in turn provide food for hunting wrens and tits.

Bird gardeners encourage ivy because it provides plenty of food as well as offering cover and a roost-place

Evergreens

Apart from food and, for some species, water as well, one of the important functions of greenery in a garden is to provide roosting shelter at night, especially in winter. So, as well as ivy, there should be plenty of other evergreens in your garden, for instance in the boundary hedge. Even laurel and rhododendron are useful in this

Treecreeper roosting in *Wellingtonia*

respect. Both common and white spruce make useful roost trees and offer good nest-sites as well. If you are lucky enough to have a *Wellingtonia*, cherish it as the preferred roost tree for tree creepers. They excavate an egg-shaped burrow in the spongy bark, then tuck themselves up for the night in a vertical posture, bill resting on the bark and tail down, feathers fluffed out boldly — a most astonishing sight. *Wellingtonia* was introduced to Britain in 1853 (the year after the Duke of Wellington died). Before this time tree creepers made hollows in rotting trees, or used natural cavities behind loose bark, as of course large numbers of them still do. But it is relatively easy to discover them on *Wellingtonia*, sometimes as many as a dozen or so, low down on the same tree.

Winter feeding

The most satisfying way to increase the bird population in your garden is by growing the right kind of plants and creating as near a wild environment for them as possible. But there is also a great deal of pleasure in providing food in the most direct manner, by setting a dining table and serving suitable dishes. And almost any food we offer, from kitchen scraps to caviar, will be eaten by a wide variety of birds ranging from tomtits to goshawks.

Importance of winter feeding

Some people say that winter bird feeding saves birds from extinction, but that isn't true. Bird numbers are mainly controlled by the availability of their natural foods; artificial feeding can have only a *small* practical effect. In really hard weather, extra feeding saves a lot of individuals from an early grave.

Sometimes people claim that it is wrong to feed birds because it interferes with the natural course of events. But we interfere in the lives of our fellow creatures and vegetation in almost everything we do, and much of this activity is perfectly proper. In any case, the provision of a measure of food and water, together with a few nestboxes, represents a modest return for the loss of natural habitat we have inflicted on our wild neighbours.

One thing is certain, if you decide to feed the birds, the best time to do it is in winter. And having started, you are honour-bound to continue until the dark days are over and your artificially maintained population is able to fend for itself in the increasingly plentiful days of spring.

Starlings and thrushes will be grateful for windfalls or any spare fruit *(A. R. Hamblin/FLPA)*

In cold weather birds fluff out their plumage in trying to keep warm; pied wagtails face hard times for there are fewer insects about

In cold weather birds face several extra problems. The ground may be so hard that they cannot get at the invertebrate creatures of the soil. Worms migrate downwards in dry or cold conditions. Days are short, so hunting time is limited. Provided that plumage is in good condition, birds are perfectly able to withstand the cold, but inevitably their energy requirement is increased as temperatures drop and they use more fuel to keep warm.

Bird tables and their siting

Ground feeders, such as blackbirds, thrushes, dunnocks and moorhens, prefer to feed at ground level, so they are best fed from a tray that is taken in at night to cheat the rats. But put the tray at least a couple of metres away from the sort of cover which might hide a stalking cat. The greatest variety of species, however, come to visit a feeding tray that is fixed a metre and a half off the ground, in a position where most of them will regard it as an unusually shaped tree branch. Tits, finches and robins will be the regular visitors, but it is possible to attract more than forty different species to a well-placed and well-stocked table.

Bird tables

Bird tables can be stuck on a post or hung from a branch or bracket. Naturally, there should be no easy access for cats. A rustic pole, of the sort all too often on sale, merely invites cats and other predators to shin up and take pot luck!

If possible, the table should be protected from hot sun and driving winds; a roof is not essential, but will keep off the worst of the rain. The tray should be cleaned often, so it is important that the coaming that frames it has a few convenient gaps to allow odds and ends to be swept away. Making a tray is easy enough. Kevin Baker illustrated a few simple designs (see page 26), but there is little doubt that the most practical bird table, offering good value for money, is the one sold by the RSPB (for address see page 93).

If you make your own, check carefully that there are no sharp edges or protruding nails. Enclosing the feeding area with chicken wire will certainly keep starlings out, but it will also keep out thrushes, doves and woodpeckers. Probably the best solution is to provide food in several ways, each allowing different birds a chance to get a share of the offerings.

The guiding principle for successful bird table operation is to offer food in an enterprising variety of ways. If the feeding station ends up looking like a Christmas tree, so much the better. Quite apart from the main dish offered on the table itself, there should be hanging baskets, seed hoppers, tit-bells and anything else you may

Some birds feed at ground level, some are happier several feet up

The RSPB bird table (left) is well designed for the benefit of birds; avoid designs like the one on the right which invites trouble by encouraging birds to nest over the communal dining room

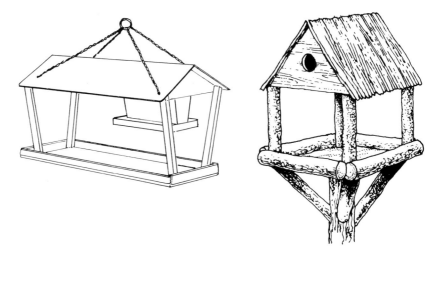

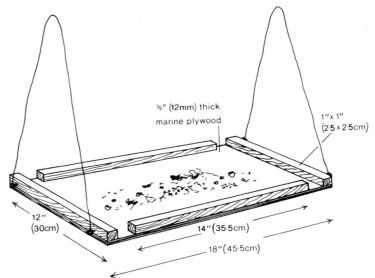

½" (12mm) thick marine plywood

1"x 1" (2·5 x 2·5 cm)

12" (30cm)

14" (35·5cm)

18" (45·5cm)

A simple bird table which may be fixed on a post or hung from a tree; the gaps in the coaming make it easier to keep clean

opposite
The RSPB bird table is well-designed, but you can easily improve it by hanging peanut bags and extras like the Trill Stick-treat *(Tony Soper)*

think of. The object is to give as wide a range of foodstuffs in as wide a range of dishes as possible. Avoid collapsible or *bouncy* spiral wire feeders though, as they may trap a bird's leg while rebounding from the shock of its arrival.

Birds will make use of convenient staging posts on their way to and from the bird table, so if there are no suitable branches, provide some substitutes in the form of posts or horizontal perches.

Bird-table foods

Animal fats, good for warblers, tits, robins, woodpeckers, nuthatches
Suet (beef best, or mutton)
Marrow bones, cracked
Bacon rinds (short pieces)
Chicken carcass (try hanging it from a tree)
Tinned pet food
Mealworms
Maggots
Ants' eggs
Cheese
Hard-boiled egg

Fruit, for thrushes, etc
  Berries of all sorts

Nuts, of all sorts
Peanuts (not salted)
Almonds
Hazel
Brazils (for nuthatches, jam them in a tree crevice)

Seeds
Mixed (ie 'Trill' brand, from shops)
Hemp (a 'best buy' — must be kept dry — eagerly taken by greenfinches, bullfinches and buntings, nuthatches, woodpeckers)
Canary (chaffinches)
Millet
Maize
Corn
Melon
Sunflower (great for greenfinches)

General
Potato (boiled or baked in jacket)
Cake crumbs
Coconut, fresh
Uncooked pastry (tree creepers like it)
Biscuit crumbs
Bread crumbs
Oats (coarse, but raw, not offered as porridge which is glutinous and sticks to plumage and bills)

Varieties of food

Different birds have different food requirements and different ways of satisfying them. This is, after all, the main reason why they manage to coexist so successfully. Therefore, the clever bird gardener studies his potential bird list and supplies and serves food accordingly. Some species are primarily vegetarian, some are seed eaters, some are carnivorous and some like a bit of everything. If you take a look at a bird's foraging tools you will straight away have a fair idea of what it needs. Finches have nutcracker bills, adapted to crack and crush, and they feed mostly on grain and seeds. They are hard-billed. Robins and wrens have slender bills designed for the delicate process of probing for grubs, caterpillars and other insects. They are soft-billed. Hawks have hooked bills for tearing flesh. Gulls have general-purpose bills.

Thrushes prefer the rich meat of worms, but will take snails or fruit as second best. Blackbirds search for worms in the first light of dawn, only later resorting to the bird table. Natural food is clearly the best for them, and if possible this is what should be provided at the feeding station. Rowan berries, elderberries, crab apples, hazel and almond nuts, boiled conkers, sweet chestnuts, acorns and beech mast are all suitable, though it will be more convenient for your guests if you crush, or chop and grate the harder nuts.

If you can go to the expense of buying commercially prepared food, then Haith's 'Songster Food' is a great success with blackbirds, robins and dunnocks (for address see page 93). Kitchen

Different feeding
methods require different
bill-shapes
1 Wren 2 Herring gull
3 Greenfinch 4 Peregrine

Song thrushes know how to crack open snail shells, but blackbirds are more aggressive and sometimes grab the meat

scraps are not only taken by the obvious 'general purpose' birds like starlings but also by the specialist insect-eaters like black-cap, chiffchaff, tree creeper, and woodpeckers.

Finches present something of a problem because they prefer seeds and seeds are expensive and extraordinarily difficult to serve without scattering. If they are offered in a mixed variety, then the birds will throw them all over the place as they search for those they like best. They also need to be kept dry, of course. Seed hoppers are notoriously ineffective, but the RSPB has produced a globe feeder which works well. It is designed to dispense peanuts or bird-seed and is constructed in such a way that seed will flow from a reservoir down to a feeding point which is easily reached by tits. Trill wild bird food is the best seed mix – birds flock to it!

Peanuts are almost the perfect product for the dedicated feeder. Convenient to handle, store and serve, they are energy-packed with a high calory content. But avoid mouldy or yellow nuts of the sort that are sometimes offered cheaply — they may be contaminated by Aflatoxin, a highly poisonous natural substance which kills a lot of birds. Unfortunately, poisonous nuts can look perfectly good to eat, so it is really most important to buy them from a reputable supplier who supports The Birdfood Standards Association (see page 93).

Unshelled peanuts will be eaten by a variety of species. Offered freely, they will be used up at the rate of several pounds a week, so it may be best to present them in bags or cages, which encourage the birds to work at the job of freeing them. Strung, in their shells, they provide entertainment for us as we watch the acrobatic tits

left
Great spotted
woodpeckers have
become fairly common
visitors to garden bird
tables; they are specially
fond of suet *(Brian
Hawkes)*

breaking and entering. But be careful that you don't string them on multi-thread cotton that might tangle up their feet. If it suits them, tits will perch on the bird table to haul up a string of nuts 'bill over claw', a version of their natural behaviour where they pull leafy twigs closer to inspect them for caterpillars.

Tits and greenfinches are the main customers for peanuts, but other species take advantage of the bits that fall to the ground. Dunnocks, and on occasion bramblings, forage below while greenfinches and as many as three species of tit are working above. Robins are fond of peanuts, too, and although they find great difficulty in fluttering alongside the mesh bag and grabbing a morsel,

It is in winter that a well-stocked bird table does its best work *(Brian Hawkes)*

In the wild siskins eat spruce and pine seeds, but garden peanut-bags have encouraged them to range further south

they can manage it. Jays, chaffinches and, indeed, bramblings, have all learnt to enjoy the bounty of the bag. One of the most remarkable instances of a bird expanding its range through a liking for peanuts is that of the siskin. This is a small acrobatic finch more closely associated with Forestry Commission conifer plantations, where they enjoy spruce and pine seeds in spring and summer. Originally confined to the Caledonian pine forest of Scotland, they slowly extended south from the mid-nineteenth century, colonising parkland and conifer forests and reaching North Wales, Norfolk and the New Forest a hundred years later. Then, some twenty years ago, they started to come into gardens and feed on peanuts in south-east England. The habit has now spread through most of the country. The numbers vary from year to year, but are generally at their highest in March and early April just before the birds migrate back to their breeding grounds — either in northern Britain or across the North Sea. Those winters when few siskins are about probably coincide with good seed crops nearer to their breeding grounds.

Scrap baskets, such as the standard RSPB wire cage, are useful because they can be filled indoors at your convenience. And the food doesn't get scattered about quite so freely as with the bird table. But, like the peanut bags, only certain birds will be able to feed from them. So, it is important to spread your offerings by way of a variety of feeding stations and devices.

Suet is a high-energy food, and it melts down well for tit-bell use. It's a good substitute for the fat grubs and insects which woodpeckers enjoy. Stuffed into mesh bags, or scrap baskets, or stuck into crevices on tree trunks, it will act as a magnet for birds like great spotted woodpeckers and long-tailed tits. If you daub suet into the crevices of an old, gnarled Scots pine, it will attract other visitors as well as the woodpeckers and treecreepers — for instance, goldcrests and even firecrests, together with wintering chiffchaffs and blackcaps.

Don't be discouraged if, after all your efforts, birds don't flock to your feast. It takes them time to adjust to a new feeding opportunity, as you will find if you move a familiar device, or paint something a new colour. Or there may be better feeding out in the surrounding countryside.

It is important to keep a bird table clean because there is an ever-present danger of bacterial infection from bird droppings (scrub with a 5 per cent bleach solution). And do not allow a pile of uneaten, unwanted food to accumulate. Move the table once or twice in a winter season to discourage a build-up of the potentially dangerous droppings on the ground.

Hard times

In extreme winter conditions, when water is frozen and mudflats are glazed by ice, water birds and waders suffer greatly. Herons and kingfishers must go down to the estuaries to find open water; pied wagtails cannot find their ditchside insects; thrushes and robins cannot penetrate the frozen earth. And small birds like long-tailed tits, wrens and goldcrests may die because there aren't enough feeding hours in the day for them to meet their high energy requirements. So, once you start operating a winter bird table, it is important that you keep it well supplied through the dark months until spring. Even then, keep feeding Trill seeds for the finches for there aren't many wild seeds about in the early part of the year.

Coal *(left)* and great tits
feeding from tit bell

Recipes

Fillings for bird bells, suet sticks and pine cones

BASIC TIT-BELL RECIPE

Fill the upturned bell with seeds, peanuts, cheese, oatmeal, sultanas, cake crumbs and other scraps. Pour in hot fat to the brim. Insert a short piece of twig into the mix to act as a learner's perch, if necessary. Leave to harden. Turn the bell over and hang in a suitable place where small birds like blue tits are already accustomed to come for food. Or tip the mix straight onto the bird table.

PINE-CONE SURPRISE

Leave a large pine cone near a fire or radiator for several days so that it opens its scales. Gather the seeds to include in the mix. Take beef suet with any meat or fat trimmings. Melt it, stir in cake crumbs, hemp, millet seeds, raisins, the pine-cone seeds, and anything else you think the birds might fancy. Pour the hot mix onto an opened cone, or dip the cone in, then allow to cool. Or stuff the holes of a feeding stick with the cooled mixture. Fix the cone or stick amongst the branches of a tree or tree substitute. An alternative to the melted suet is peanut butter.

Cakes and puddings for the bird table

BASIC PUDDING

8oz (200g) beef suet, 12oz (300g) coarse oatmeal, 2-3oz (50-75g) flour, 5oz (125g) water

Mix flour and oatmeal with liquid fat and water to stiff paste. Bake in shallow pie dish to form flat cake at 175°C (350°F/Reg 4) for approximately one hour.

MAIZE CAKE

Mix 3oz (75g) maize in a bowl with equal quantities of chopped nuts, hemp, canary and millet seed. Stir with boiling water till coagulated, and add two beaten eggs. Tie tightly in a cloth and bake at 175°C (350°F/Reg 4) for fifty minutes to one hour.

BIRD CAKE

2lb (1kg) flour (wholemeal best), 8oz (200g) margarine, a little sugar

Mix with water and bake like a rock bun.

CHAPTER THREE

Birds need Water as well

Food isn't enough, there's drinking and bathing too . . .

A HEALTHY bird needs a supply of clean fresh water, partly because it will drink some, but mostly because it bathes a lot. Birds don't sweat. If they get overheated they open their mouths wide and gape to lose heat, losing moisture at the same time. They also lose moisture in their droppings, and this must be replaced. Tree-living species may sip from foliage after rain. For them, provide a drinking bowl well off the ground. Many town birds happily visit roof gutters to drink and bathe.

Most birds drink by dipping their bills into the water, then raising their heads to allow the liquid to run down their throats. But pigeons keep their bills in the water, sucking it up and into the system in bulk, a method which is quick and leaves the bird at risk for the shortest time. Swallows, martins and swifts will drink in flight in a shower of rain, or from the surface of the pond. And, like other birds, they enjoy bathing in the rain or even flying through the spray of a lawn sprinkler. However, they will be cautious of bathing in a downpour, since the object of bathing is to wet the plumage but not to soak it.

Birds do not only bathe in water. On occasion they will enjoy sun, rain, snow, smoke and dust baths, and they will even bathe in ants. These are all different forms of feather maintenance.

Bird baths and their maintenance

The sides of bird baths are often too steep and the water too deep. Three inches (7.5cm) should be the maximum depth, and the access should be by a gradual non-slip slope. Birds like to wade in

Even an old dustbin lid
can make a useful bird
bath

cautiously. If you have a bird bath which has a slippery, or glazed surface, put in some sand or gravel to make life easier for them.

If the bird bath contains no oxygenating vegetation it must be cleaned frequently, or there will be a build up of algae which will stink. The water should be changed frequently (daily in hot weather) and must be kept topped up. It is best set up in shade, in the open but within reach of cover and safety.

Ponds

A pond is almost essential for a good bird garden. Properly stocked with oxygenating plants and supporting a healthy population of aquatic insects, snails and crustaceans it will provide clean water for drinking and bathing as well as a useful food supply. As anyone with a pond will tell you, it is also an endless source of delight.

How to make a small pond

MATERIAL LIST:
a pond liner, 8ft 3in x 6ft 6in (2.5m x 2m)
ten wooden stakes
mallet
piece of timber, 6ft 6in x 2ft 6in x 2in (2m x 75cm x 50mm)
spirit level
spade
sand or newspaper

The pond liner may be bought from a water garden or plastics supplier, but avoid anything less than 1,000 gauge [15/1000] (0.375

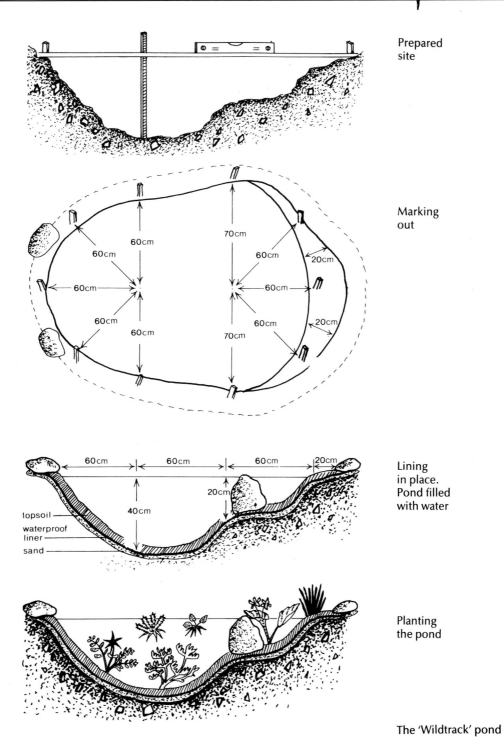

Prepared site

Marking out

60cm
60cm
70cm
60cm
60cm
60cm
60cm
20cm
60cm
60cm
60cm
60cm
60cm
20cm
60cm
70cm

Lining
in place.
Pond filled
with water

60cm   60cm   60cm   20cm

20cm

40cm

topsoil
waterproof
liner
sand

Planting
the pond

The 'Wildtrack' pond

Birds need water for drinking as well as bathing; blackbird at a pool *(Eric & David Hosking)*

Cock chaffinch bathing, part of the ritual of feather maintenance *(Roger Tidman/FLPA)*

microns) thick as it is easily punctured. There are several kinds:

black polythene — cheapest type, but has a limited life of about five years unless protected from sunlight by covering of earth and stones.

PVC sheeting — more expensive but more resistant to sunlight, best type strengthened with nylon.

polyolefin — a high grade plastic liner with a life of over fifteen years.

butyl rubber — a very flexible rubber liner with a life of over fifteen years. The best quality liner but the most expensive.

If you choose to line your pond with concrete it should be at least 6in (15cm) thick and must be sealed with bituminous paint or waterseal cement.

METHOD:

1   Mark out the edges of the pond with stakes. If the ground is not quite level, put the shallow end at the bottom of the slope. Hammer in a stake at each end of the pond using measurements on the diagram (see page 37). (It's important to keep to these or the liner will not fit.) Rest the wooden beam across the two stakes and mark a point on the beam 2ft (60cm) in from each stake. You can find the position of the other stakes by measuring out from these points.

2   You can now start to dig the hole. Put any turves to one side as

A garden pond will be used both for drinking and bathing, but it also provides a lot of food

House sparrows have learnt to dunk stale bread in water

you can use them later to fringe the pond. Save the topsoil as well, because this will be put back in the finished pond. The best of the soil could be used to make a bank. Put soil to one side, out of the way of the spread lining.

3   As soon as the hole begins to grow, check that the sides are at the same level by laying the wooden beam over it and checking with the spirit level. Take out the stakes and remove the earth from the higher sides.

4   Use the diagram to work out the different depths of the pond. The deepest part of the pond is a third of the way from the end, and the sides should shelve up gradually from this point to the edge. Do not make the slope too steep. Check the depths are right by measuring down from the wooden beam. If you dig too deep don't worry — you can always put some back.

5   A special feature of the pond is the marshy area at the shallow end. Extend it by removing earth to a depth of 2in (5cm) for a distance of 8in (20cm) away from that end.

6   When the hole is ready, pick out any stones or sticks that might puncture the lining and carefully pour some damp sand to make a layer ¾in (2cm) deep over the whole of the pond. This is to give a soft base for the lining to rest on. If you prefer, you can use sheets of spread-out newspaper, but make sure you build up a good layer.

7   Take the liner, and with it, overlap the deep end of the pond by 8in (20cm). Anchor it with heavy stones, temporarily.

8   Spread out the liner over the pond, and push it gently down into the hole. Don't try to make it fit too snugly as the weight of the water will do that.

9   Fill the pond almost to the top with water. You can now see whether you've made any mistakes in levelling the pond. Any errors can be put right by removing or adding earth under the liner. Make sure that there are going to be water levels of from ¾in to 4in (2cm to 10cm) at the shallow end.

10   You should wait two or three days to allow the liner to settle, then carefully trim off the surplus plastic round the edge leaving at least 8in (20cm) overlap, but do not cut any off at the shallow end. Do not trim too soon, the weight of the water drags in a lot of slack. And do not trim too close, or you will have difficulties when arranging your pond surround of stones or turf.

11   Secure the edges of the plastic by burying it under earth or large stones. You can also use the turf for this. If you are using a

polythene liner it's very important to ensure that the sheet is totally buried, as in time the sunlight will destroy it.

12 Take the topsoil you have saved and sprinkle it over the surface of the pool until you have built up a layer of silt several inches deep over the liner. The earth will form a marshy area at the shallow end. This earth should not be in contact with the surrounding ground or in dry weather water will be drawn out of the pond by capillary action.

13 Take a couple of large stones, and place them in the shallow end so that they show above the surface. Birds will use these as perching places.

Pond plants

The pond must be properly stocked with suitable plants for it to establish a healthy home for a living community. The plants release oxygen into the water and absorb the carbon dioxide produced by the water animals that are bound to colonise it. The plants also provide food, shade and shelter for the animals. They thrive on plenty of light, but welcome protection from strong winds. There are three main plant categories, and you should make certain your pond is stocked with some of each.

1 **Free-floating plants** live at the surface, with their roots suspended in the water, eg *Hydrocharis morsus-ranae*; water soldier, *Stratiotes aloides*; duckweed, *Lemna sp.*; *Hottonia palustris*, water violet — whose flowers are rich with nectar and attract pollinating insects.

2 **Oxygenators** live fully submerged in the deeper part of the pool, some rooted to the mud at the bottom. They are vital, eg starwort, *Callitriche autumnalis*; water milfoil, *Myriophyllum sp*; hornwort, *Ceratophyllum demersum*. The starwort is especially valuable because it retains its oxygenating properties throughout the winter. Quillwort, *Isoetes lacustris*, is an excellent food plant from the point of view of fish.

3 **Marginals** live in marshy areas at the edge of the pond and have most of their foliage above water, eg water forget-me-not, *Myosotis sp*; brook-lime, *Veronica beccabunga*; marsh marigold, *Caltha palustris*; flowering rush, *Butomus umbellatus*; slender spike-rush, *Eleocharis acicularis* (this may survive submerged but will then be sterile).

Ponds need to be planted with oxygenators like, for instance, the common water starwort

Even a small pond will attract birds — starlings in this case (*A. R. Hamblin/ FLPA*)

Magpies are becoming more common in gardens (*Peggy Heard/FLPA*)

Birds do not only drink water! Blue tits long ago learnt how to steal the cream from milk bottles (*Brian Hawkes*)

Looking after feathers

The care of feathers is a critical part of every bird's daily maintenance programme. However cold it is on a winter's day or however insistently the young family calls for food in the summer, sometime the vital business of preening and keeping the feathers in good condition must be fitted in. As well as giving birds the power of flight, its feathers are also the means of insulating and helping to control the body temperature. Bedraggled feathers waste body heat and make for inefficient flying, and in winter lost body heat is not easily replaced. The first key to this servicing of feathers is regular bathing, followed up by re-proofing and finishing off with careful manicuring.

The bird bath and the garden pond are focal points in the bird's daily life and they will be used more in the holidays of July and August than at any other time. Birds bathe energetically, splashing and shaking themselves in the water until the plumage is thoroughly wetted. The aim is to wet the plumage without actually soaking it, there-fore making it more receptive to the oiling and preening that follow. Water is splashed well into the feathers to wash out the dust, scales and parasites that accumu-late there. The water is then squeezed to the surface and shaken off as the bird dries itself.

The blackbird is a great bather; watch it as it shows off the feathers to best advan-tage at bathing time; with wings outspread the handsome tail is held down at a right angle and fanned wide to show its full spread.

Once the bathing is finished the bird be-gins to preen. Twisting its tail to one side it reaches down over its back and collects the waterproofing oil with its bill from the preen gland near the base of its tail then carefully wipes the oil onto its body feath-ers and wings. In between times it will take individual feathers in its bill and very gently stroke them back into shape, zip-ping together the individual barbs and tiny barbules that have been ruffled and dis-placed during the day's activities.

Robin bathing; birds *need* water to help them
keep their feathers in trim

It is best to buy pest-free stock from a nurseryman. Follow his instructions in planting. But a general rule is to put the marginals in water 1in to 4in (2.5cm to 10cm) deep, rooting them in good topsoil. The oxygenators will grow in water 6in to 24in (15cm to 60cm) deep; if they need planting (as *Myriophyllum*, for instance), the best method is to use the specially made baskets which are cheap to buy and allow you to make changes easily.

Pond animals and visitors

Animals will find their own way to your pond, but it makes sense to introduce some common water snails straightaway, for they will serve a useful purpose in grazing the algae. Buy them from your aquarist, and remember that cheap ones eat just as much as expensive ones. Ramshorn snails, *Planorbis corneus*, or the freshwater winkle, *Paludina vivipare*, are the species least likely to attack your 'best' plants. One snail to every 2sq in (5sq cm) of surface water is about right, but don't put too many in; they will soon find their own balance.

Dragonflies like ponds

You may want to introduce frogs (by way of spawn clouds in the spring), toads (spawn strings), water spiders and beetles.

If you have a big enough pond you may be able to attract wild duck, like these teal

Birds must bathe even when there is snow on the ground, because it helps them to keep their feathers in trim, thus keeping them warm; this song thrush is going to a bath that is kept ice-free by the nightlight in the tin beneath *(Brian Hawkes)*

But avoid the great diving beetle, *Dytiscus marginalis*, if you are going to have fish, because it will attack them. And avoid newts in a small pond for they will eat almost anything. Most insect species will find their own way — for instance, dragonflies, water boatmen and pond skaters. Sticklebacks and minnows will control the mosquito and gnat larvae that will inevitably appear. Again, a rough rule of thumb is 1in (2.5cm) of fish to 24sq in (60sq cm) of surface area. But it is best not to have fish in a very small pond.

The pond should need little maintenance. When it is first filled and planted it will probably be opaque and green-looking for several weeks, but as the plants grow the water will clear. In hot weather you may have to add water, especially if you are losing it by capillary action. Devise some way of trickle-feeding it, or diverting rain to it, to save a great deal of trouble. If it is near trees, then fallen leaves will need to be removed in the autumn, but it should not be necessary to clean the pond out completely. With well-balanced populations a pond will stay healthy for years.

CHAPTER FOUR

Somewhere to Nest

Your birds are well-fed and watered; now they're house hunting . . .

SOME BIRDS nest in holes and some don't. Tits, nutchatches, starlings, tree sparrows and woodpeckers, for instance, live in secret caverns and crevices; robins, blackbirds and spotted fly-catchers live out in the open, but for all that they are well hidden. Rooks and herons don't bother to conceal their nests, and instead site them at a safe distance off the ground. Most seabirds, waders and waterfowl live out in the open for all to see, yet carefully choose places where they will be undisturbed — high cliffs, remote places or islands.

Most woodland is managed for maximum timber production, and decaying trees are not tolerated. So there is a chance for the bird gardener to redress the balance if he or she can allow an old and dying tree to live out its time undisturbed. Hedges offer plenty of prime building sites for birds, especially when they are prickly enough to discourage predators. Hawthorn and holly are both excellent. Layered and trimmed, they provide dense cover for robins, dunnock, wrens, linnets, greenfinches and chaffinches, whitethroats and blackbirds, and so on. Beech and yew hedges also serve well, and although they are not prickly, they are still difficult to penetrate. Very often their usefulness can be improved by pruning to make forked sites about 5ft (1.5m) above the ground. Prune in autumn or winter to avoid disturbance at breeding time. Cracks and crannies in sheds and stone walls are to be encouraged, providing near-natural homes for tits and wagtails. On an outside wall the ivy and honeysuckle grown for their food potential also give nesting possibilities in the breeding season for such as spotted flycatchers and blackbirds. Sometimes it is possible to take out a brick or two from a wall and enlarge the hole behind it to make a welcome for a

Spotted flycatchers like to nest against a creeper-clad wall

pied wagtail. Blackbirds will come indoors to a little-used shed and build on a shelf, as will swallows and robins. They all like to nest up *against* something — an old can or box perhaps. The cracks, crannies and wall ledges will be variously seen by different species as versions of their natural tree holes or sea cliff ledges. So enlarge holes to 1⅛in (29mm) for tits, and ensure there are larger entrance holes, always open, so that swallows and other birds can find their way into the garage or potting shed.

There are endless possibilities for creating natural and near-natural nest sites and it is really more a question of improvisation than anything else, based on a study of the bird's natural requirements. Obviously it is important to avoid a situation in which a bird's home may be too easily discovered. And don't improve a site that has already been successful.

Nestboxes are readily available from commercial suppliers (see the advertisements in the RSPB magazine *Birds*, and the birdwatchers' monthly magazine, *British Birds*). But it's easy to make your own. Tit boxes are the most successful. The drawing shows how to mark up a piece of boarding, 41in x 6in (104cm x 15cm), to cut out the pieces for one standard box. The ¾in (18mm) timber is thick enough to afford good insulation and to last a reasonable length of time. Softwood such as old floorboarding is usually the right size and is well seasoned and ideal. The interior size is critical. In the case of great and blue tits the floor area should be at least 4in x 4in (100mm x 100mm). In the plan, we have allowed for a more generous 6in x 4½in (15cm x 11.5cm). If the floor is larger than this the tits have to import lots of material to form foundations for the nestcup. You may feel the dimensions of the interior of the box are surprisingly small, but the incubating bird squats in a small space, and there is no need to accommodate their stretched length. Also, when the chicks are hatched they will benefit from the warmth of a close jumble of bodies, provided there is enough room for them to stretch their wings.

For hole nesters, like tits, the entrance must definitely not be at floor level. The birds need to import a quantity of nest material, which will occupy a space at the bottom of the box, and in any case the chicks would be extra vulnerable to predators if there was an opening at their nestcup level. The single entrance hole must be

In autumn, when leaves fall from deciduous trees and shrubs, old nests will be very easy to spot among the bare branches — nests that you may not have suspected were there during the breeding season!

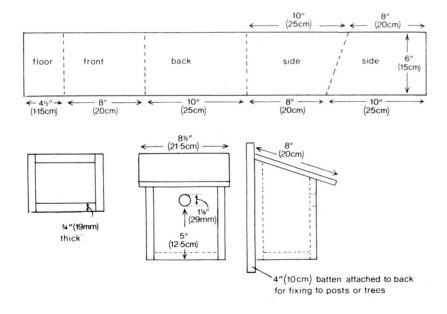

Exploded view of the basic tit-box

near the top, on any side, at least 5in (12.5cm) from the floor, thus containing the nestlings and discouraging any cats' paws which might fish them out. Tits prefer a very small entrance hole, another feature which makes theft difficult for cats. A 1⅛in (29mm)-diameter hole will allow easy access for both blue and great tits. Don't be tempted to increase the size of the hole when you see birds pecking at the entrance. They are not trying to make it larger in order to get in more easily — tits just tend to peck at anything. If the holes are too large, incidentally, nuthatches will plaster them with mud to reduce them to a size which suits.

A treecreeper nestbox acts as a substitute for the kind of nest cavity made by a piece of bark that is peeling away from the tree trunk *(Brian Hawkes)*

Do not include any kind of perch, intended to allow the incoming or outgoing bird a place to rest and fold its wings before it negotiates the hole. Study of movie film has shown that they close their wings with great facility in order to pass through, and the exterior of the box is a dangerous place where they have no desire to wait about. Perches only serve to make life easier for cats and weasels. But there does need to be a clear, uncluttered flight path to the hole, giving room for the spread of full wingspan right up to the entrance.

Nestbox construction does not need to be to a high standard of carpentry. The completed work must be windproof and rainproof, and if this means liberal use of sealants the birds will not complain. A poor fit around floor level has the advantage of providing vital water drainage.

Siting the box is critical. The main considerations are protection from the elements and from enemies. First consider the lifestyle of the intended occupant when you choose a place for it. Tit boxes should be attached to walls or trees, which is where they will be looking for likely entrance holes. The open plan boxes for blackbirds, robins, and spotted flycatchers should be placed against a wall where they are hidden in a dense jungle of ivy or some other creeper, or in a thick hedge, or in a fruit tree where there is some cover. They are best fixed in discreet crotch sites, invisible to the outside world. The birds will find them.

Most garden nestboxes should be fixed at about 5ft to 6ft (1.5m to 1.8m) above the ground. Factors such as possible disturbance will obviously affect the decision, and it is worth remembering that birds will nest at heights ranging from ground level to tree top. To protect them from hot sun and wet Atlantic winds, the general rule is that the opening should face somewhere in the arc from north through east to south-east but, if it is well sheltered, this question of orientation is probably not significant. Nestboxes do not need to be hidden away in a dense clump of trees, or in the middle of a vast woodland. It is better to site them at the edge of a copse, or shrubbery, where the grass and trees meet.

This is the kind of country that gives the best feeding return. A convenient staging post some 6ft (1.8m) away may be an asset. This can be anything from a clothes line to a twig.

Firm fixing for nestboxes is not really necessary; after all, birds often build nests in places which sway with the wind. Even boxes that literally hang from tree branches are successful. But for all that it makes good sense to fix a box *securely*, and no one, least of all the occupant, wants it to collapse because of an inadequate screw or rusty nail. And fix the box by way of a batten, which will help to ensure that it does not become permanently wet and fall apart. Many clutches are drowned in natural nest-sites every year, so take particular care to see that rainwater cannot find its way into the box. Remember that a lot of rain trickles down a wall or tree trunk, and it tends to follow well established channels. Make sure the box stands proud of them, or to one side. Incline the box outwards with a slight slant, so that drips from the projecting roof do not go through the entrance hole. Do not worry if the floor of the box, when set up, is not quite horizontal. The birds will solve this problem if they need to, when they import nest material.

Songbird nestboxes may be 'primed' with a layer of moss or a plaited ring of straw, to make them even more attractive to house-hunters, but this is unlikely to be an important consideration in determining whether the box will be 'bought' or not.

As with robins, and indeed many other species, it is the male blue tit who has the job of finding likely sites and he then takes the female to see them. She chooses, then cleans it in preparation for nest building. The cleaning may not be very thorough, and frequently she will simply build on top of an old nest. The corners will

Swifts collect nest material in flight such as down and feathers

Eggs

Birds may lay eggs at any time of year, but cold weather and the scarcity of food allow very few winter families to survive. Natural selection will always ensure that most birds nest when food is most freely available. Indeed even the size of the clutch is regulated by the available food; in cold or drought fewer eggs are laid. Conditions may have improved by the time the eggs hatch, but the birds don't have any way of foreseeing this when they lay. First-time breeders also lay fewer eggs. And something which may surprise many people is that farmland and woodland pairs lay more eggs on average than garden birds, because suburban feeding is less satisfactory, though it may be generous.

be filled and a foundation of mosses and grasses laid. Not surprisingly, birds tend to make use of the building materials most conveniently to hand (or beak). Nests in trees tend to be made of twigs, those in cliffs of seaweed and driftwood, on beaches of pebbles, on moorland of heather. And in a factory — bits of wire!

If you provide suitable materials, birds will collect them. In the breeding season, when the scrap and peanut cages are not required for food, they can be packed with straw, cotton-wool, sheep wool, etc. In the garden, this may reduce the amount of thieving the sparrows and jackdaws will indulge in when they try to unravel the string from your bean poles, or tease out threads from your clothes on the washing line. Tree species will prefer your offerings to be hung from the branches. But put some at ground level, in a mesh bag perhaps, firmly pegged so that they can't be carried away in bulk.

If the weather is particularly dry in May, when the house martins are busy plastering their nestcups, it may be helpful to pour a couple of buckets of water over the earth in a likely place, eg along a dusty country lane or over a bare patch on the lawn or in a park. They sometimes have difficulty finding mud puddles from which to pick up their nest gobbets.

If you *are* lucky enough to be successful in enticing a breeding pair to your nestbox, keep any inspection to a minimum. Be thoughtful with your photography, and in particular be extremely sensitive with any 'gardening' you may be tempted to do with

Don't fix a perch to your nestbox; birds fly straight in, so it only makes life easier for thieving weasels

Early Man-made Nestboxes

The earliest artificial nest sites were pigeon-holes designed to attract rock pigeons; at Port Eynon, on the Gower coast, there is an early pigeon-house formed when a natural cliff crevice was walled in *(Tony Soper)*

Eighteenth-century French dovecotes were sometimes highly decorated and impressive but the purpose was utilitarian — the production of a regular supply of fat squabs for the kitchen *(Tony Soper)*

The interior of a typically Norman dovecote has five hundred or more pigeon-holes and an ingenious device called a potence that allows the pigeon-keeper to reach any of his birds from a revolving ladder *(Tony Soper)*

natural nests which don't quite suit your angle of view. You may, inadvertently, betray the nest to a predator. If you are recording the story of your nests for the British Trust for Ornithology's Nest Record Scheme (see page 84) keep your visits to a minimum. The wellbeing and safety of the birds is paramount — put their interests first. If you want to count the young, wait a few days from hatching in the case of small birds. And don't creep up on the nest with exaggerated fairy footsteps. Better to let them know you're coming. It is also important not to disturb nests at the stage when their occupants are close to leaving, since there is a danger they might 'explode' away and become exposed too soon to the attention of the world at large. However, if this disaster should occur, collect up the chicks in a handkerchief as best you may and post them back home. Then block up the entrance for ten minutes or so, until they have quietened down.

Unhatched eggs, dead or disappearing juveniles, are a sad possi-

Pied flycatchers are very keen on nestboxes

bility. Any number of causes may account for them, apart from the natural loss to predators. A dead parent, inexperienced first-time parents who may have failed in their duty, shortage of food at a critical time — all are possibilities. Double check to see whether rainwater, or cold winds or the sun's heat, or a cat perch, were responsible. And if you are reasonably certain the fault was not yours, reflect that a natural event of this kind is the normal end for an enormous number of nestlings. It is part of the expected scheme of things.

At the end of the breeding season, in say September and October (but remember that some species, even tits very occasionally, raise more than one brood), remove the used nests and give the boxes an anti-bug spray. The nests and box crevices will be home for feather lice, mites, ticks and flea larvae — creatures that can survive long periods without their host — so you will need to dust with some safe insecticide. A squirt of pyrethrum dust would do the job, or perhaps an end-of-season coat of creosote or Cuprinol. Then it will be ready for a winter let. Moths may overwinter in them, perhaps even toads, mice or bats. Great and blue tits will certainly use them

Like the other crows, magpies are egg thieves and they are much more common in gardens, where they are not persecuted

Wrens use nestboxes as winter roost-places

or winter warmth, roosting in solitary splendour. They often take to centrally-heated street lamps for overnight roosts. House martins, which frequently produce three broods of young and whose breeding season can then extend into November, roost in family parties in their nest cavities, which must make for a tight fit.

Give the boxes a spring clean before the breeding season, cleaning out any droppings left by the winter occupants, and another squirt of pyrethrum will kill the bugs.

Among the many summer birds that descend on our gardens in April is the cheery house martin, which arrives during the second half of the month. It has flown from West Africa, making a fast crossing of the Sahara at high level, unlike the more punishing low-level passage the swallows take, wasting vital energy searching for non-existent insects on the way. As soon as the house martins

House martin feeding
young at an artificial nest
(Brian Hawkes)

Tree sparrows are the
'country cousins' of
house sparrows *(Brian
Hawkes)*

arrive last year's nests are inspected; most of them are probably still intact and securely tucked up tight under the eaves. Necessary repairs are put in hand almost immediately. The house martin is one of the great mud-nest builders and cements its cup-shaped home firmly against the wall; with luck each nest will stay there for several years and need little repairing. One of the martin's many endearing habits is that it likes to go to new houses on suburban estates and will often colonise them almost before people move in. In years when April and May are very dry the martins may be hard pressed to find mud, so it is worth watching for this and lending a hand by providing muddy puddles at their usual collection points if needed.

These birds will readily take to artificial nests and if you want to attract them to your house it is well worth trying to do so. Although you can make perfectly good nests yourself out of Polyfilla (or cement and sawdust if you have nimble fingers) it is much easier and not too expensive to buy them off the shelf. Nerine Nurseries, Welland, Malvern, Worcestershire WR13 6LN are good suppliers and the RSPB also sells them. The nests are easily fixed under eaves or below upstairs window sills and act as good starter homes to provide the foundation for a colony. They are most likely to be taken up if another colony already exists nearby. These artificial nests are fixed on cuphooks and can be easily lifted off to inspect the contents. It seems that they may be more successful on the north or east walls of buildings.

House sparrows sometimes gatecrash the house martin nests, either before the owners return from their winter in the sun or by

House martins originally plastered their mud huts on cliff and cave overhangs but nowadays they colonise the eaves of houses; if you put up the artificial nests, sometimes the birds will add their own mud ones *(Brian Hawkes)*

Some nestbox questions:

When is the box
  first visited — by
  one bird or two?
Can you tell the
  sexes apart?
How do they
  behave towards
  each other? —
  other birds? —
  people?
What sounds are
  made?
When is the first
  material brought
  in?
What is used?
Does the nature of
  the material
  change during the
  building?
How many visits
  per hour, per day,
  in all?
Does the rate of
  work vary?
How is the work
  shared?
What food is
  brought?
By one adult or
  both?
How often?
What calls are used?
When do young
  leave the nest?
Are they still being
  fed?
How long do they
  stay around?
Is the nest clean?
  — why?
What is it made of?

ousting them once they have repaired the nests. To prevent this happening, hang a series of weighted strings no more than 12in (30cm) in length and 6in (15cm) away from the entrance holes and at 2½in (6cm) intervals. House martins approach the nests steeply from below and will pass freely behind the strings. The sparrows, with their level-flight approach, will be deterred by the strings.

Later in the season it is quite possible that a heavily loaded mud nest may break off the wall and spill the fledglings on the ground below. Get to them before the neighbour's cat and put them in a small open-top box, or an old blackbird nest or similar. Then climb up a ladder and fix the box or nest containing the young to the wall close to the site they fell from. There is every possibility that the parents will rear them successfully.

Some people object to the pile of droppings below a house martin colony, especially if it is over a doorway or open window. The problem can easily be solved by fixing a 9in (22cm) board some 6ft (1.8cm) below the nests to trap the droppings. Either make the shelf removable on keyhole brackets, or use a ladder to clean it at the end of the season. Under the 1981 Wildlife and Countryside Act it is illegal to take, damage or destroy a house martin's nest while it is in use.

Nestboxes for other birds that you might be able to attract to your garden, given the right conditions, are described in the following pages, together with a little information about the birds to help you look for them in their natural habitat. (For comprehensive information on all the nestboxing birds see *The Bird Table Book*: Tony Soper, David & Charles 1986).

Do not disturb the sitting bird in your nestbox in case you betray it to a predator

Nestboxes

ROBIN   *Erithacus rubecula*
Resident and generally distributed, except in extreme north of Scotland. Gardens, hedgerows, woods with undergrowth.

Nests in gardens and hedgerows in bankside hollows, tree holes, walls, amongst creeper, on shelves in outbuildings, often at foot of bush or grassy tuft. Foundation of dried leaves and moss, neatly lined with hair and perhaps a feather or two.

Nestbox: ledge or tray, open-fronted box. Interior floor at least 4in x 4in (10cm x 10cm). Old tin, watering can, or kettle, at least quart-size, well shaded from sun, spout down for drainage. Fix it about 5in (1.5m) up in a strong fork site. Prime with a plaited circle of straw.

Eggs: Usually 5-6 white, with sandy or reddish freckles. Late March to July. Incubation 13-14 days; fledging 12-14 days. Two or more broods.

MALLARD   *Anas platyrhynchos*
Generally distributed, near all kinds of freshwater, estuaries and coastal islands.

Nests in thick undergrowth sometimes far from water. Pollard willows, tree holes, second-hand crow nests, etc. Grass, leaves, rushes, feathers, down.

Nestbox: try to provide an apple-box or large, open cat basket in typical nesting area. Where mallards have become very tame (village ponds and the like), erect an open-ended barrel on an island. Otherwise a mere hollow in the ground, bordered by a couple of short logs and sheltering under a wigwam of spruce boughs, may do the trick. Mallard nests are probably best sited on rafts or islands, where they enjoy some protection from foxes and rats.

Alternative nestbox: using sawmill offcuts, make a box with inside dimensions of 1ft (30cm) square and 9in (23cm) high. Prime with an inch or two (25cm to 50cm) of

Robins may nest in an old kettle, but make sure the
spout points down so that water drains away

left
Starlings take readily to nestboxes but they need a 2in (50mm) entrance hole, so a titbox defeats them until the wood has softened enough for them to open out the hole *(Brian Hawkes)*

right
The farmyard won't get swept for a month till the blackbird fledges its young *(Brian Hawkes)*

below
Robins nest in an astonishing variety of sites *(Eric & David Hosking)*

woodshavings. Make a funnel about a foot (30cm) long leading to an entrance hole 6in (15cm) square. This tunnel entrance serves to deter crows. A ramp should lead gently down from the tunnel entrance to the ground. This ease of access is important, not only for the comfort of the duck, but because she might take broods back to the safety of the box at night for the first couple of weeks after leaving the nest, especially in cold weather. NB: A duck-box may well be taken over by moorhens.

Eggs: About 12 greyish-green or greenish-buff, occasionally a clear pale blue. February onwards. Incubation 4 weeks; fledging 7½ weeks. One or two broods.

KESTREL *Falco tinnunculus*

Resident, generally distributed, except in winter in far north. Moors, coast, farmland and open woodland, suburbs and cities.

Makes no nest, but uses a scrape on cliff or quarry ledge or uses second-hand crow nest as platform. Sometimes in tree hollow or ledge on building or ruin.

Nestbox: open-fronted, 25in x 15in x 15in (63.5cm x 38cm x 38cm) high, with roof overhanging a couple of inches (5cm). One of the long sides is partly open, having only a 5in (12.5cm) board along the bottom part, fitted with a broom pole lip to enable the bird to perch easily before entering. Prime the box with some peat mould or woodshavings. Fix very firmly on 18ft to 30ft (6m to 10m approx) pole, or high on side of house where some shelter is available from midday sun. If fixed to tree, make sure chick thieves cannot climb to it easily (there is a ready illegal market for juvenile kestrels). And place it so that wing-exercising juveniles can step out onto a branch.

In Holland, where farmers erect these boxes to encourage kestrels in controlling voles and shrews, they have been highly successful.

Eggs: About 5, the white colour often hidden by red-brown splotchings. Mid April onwards. Incubation 28 days; fledging 28 days. One brood.

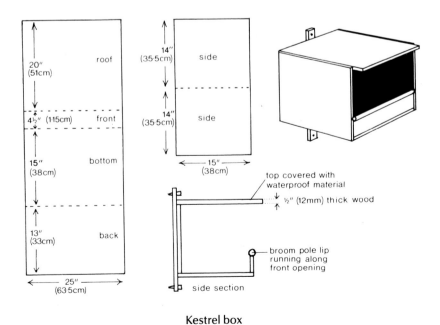

Kestrel box

BLACKBIRD *Turdus merula*

Resident and generally distributed. Woods, hedges, gardens, shrubberies.

Nests in hedges, bushes, evergreens, ivy, sometimes in outhouses. Sturdily built of grasses, roots, etc. Inner mud cup lined with grasses.

Nestbox: tray or open-fronted, with a floor area 12in x 12in (30cm x 30cm). Or try an inverted cone made of roofing felt. Cut into circle 9in (23cm) in diameter. Cut out and throw away a V-shaped sector from centre to a 2in (5cm) arc at the outside edge. Cut a 1in (2.5cm) section from centre (to provide drainage). Now overlap open ends 3in (7.5cm) and staple strongly. Resulting cone is approx 7in (17.5cm) in diameter with a depth of 2in (5cm). Or try a bundle of pea sticks arranged with a central cave.

Eggs: 4-5 bluish-green, freckled with red-brown. February (or even earlier) to July. Incubation 13-14 days; fledging 13-14 days.

Two or three broods, the first often being vandalised because it is insufficiently concealed by leaves, later broods being more successful. Five broods have been raised in one season.

SPOTTED FLYCATCHER

Muscicapa striata

Summer resident, generally distributed. Gardens, parks, woodland edges.

Nests against wall or on small ledge supported by creeper or fruit trees, etc. Moss and grass, lined with wool, hair or feathers.

Nestbox: ledge or open fronted box with at least 3in x 3in (7.5cm x 7.5cm) floor. Hide one of those bowl-shaped wire flower baskets in dense honeysuckle, primed with some moss. Have a perch not far away.

Eggs: 4-5 greenish-grey, with brown spots. Mid May to June. Incubation 12-13; fledging 12-13 days. One brood.

Spotted flycatchers may
take over a hanging plant basket

Spotted flycatchers find a
hanging flower basket
ideal for a nest site *(Brian
Hawkes)*

Spotted flycatchers nest
in the corner of an old
shed *(Eric & David
Hosking)*

An old wicker chair may
not improve the
appearance of a village
pond but it makes a
convenient spot for a
moorhen's nest *(Brian
Hawkes)*

BARN OWL   Tyto alba

Resident, generally distributed but not abundant and decreasing. Vicinity of farms, old buildings, church towers, etc. Parkland with old timber.

Nests in ruins or unoccupied buildings, hollow trees and cliff crevices. No material used, the eggs are often surrounded by a pile of cast pellets.

Nestbox: barn owls are a beneficial species from the point of view of farmers, hunting a diet of short tailed voles, common shrews and wood mice. Formerly much persecuted by the ignorant, they have been further declining in this century because of habitat loss and human disturbance. But there is also a chronic shortage of suitable nest sites such as old trees, derelict buildings and old-style brick and timber barns. Modern steel-framed barns offer no home to nesting barn owls. Fortunately, they take readily to nestboxes, particularly if the box is placed in a building which is not too often disturbed.

There are several designs, and it may be necessary to use a good deal of skill in fitting the box to the site. The RSPB suggests that enclosed storage barns with access

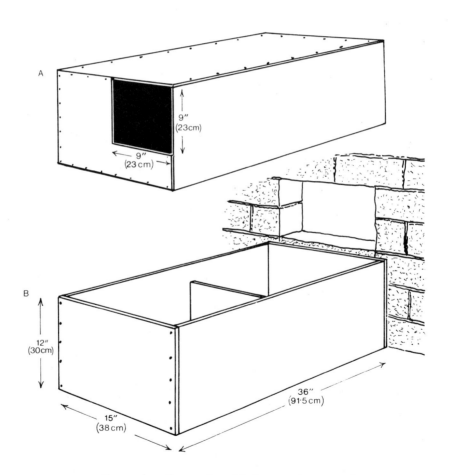

Barn owl nestboxes; type A is for a modern open barn, type B for enclosed barns which have an access hole in the gable end

from outside are most favoured, but open Dutch barns are also suitable, particularly if the nestbox can be secured to beams or struts and used for roosting in winter. This will increase the chance of nesting the following year.

The design of the boxes is quite straightforward, as they can easily be made from a standard tea chest or packing case — both for lightness and ease of conversion they are hard to beat. If you can find a source of supply, wooden barrels are also easy to convert. Tea chests and packing cases, however, are not waterproof and should only be sited in dry locations. If the nestboxes are exposed to the elements, more durable and water-resistant material must be used. The lining papers and metal edging around the top of the chest must be removed and any nails knocked flat. You will also need some wooden trays — baker's trays are ideal — which are sawn in half to provide two platforms of about 18in (45cm) in depth. These are important as they provide a safe area in front of the box where the young can come out and stretch their wings.

It is easiest to erect a nestbox in a timber barn — a steel-trussed building may require considerable dexterity. The most important parts to remember are that the boxes must be secure inside the barn, as high above the ground as possible, in the darkest corner out of any draughts and where there is permanent access for the birds. Since height is one of the main criteria, the easiest time to put up the boxes is when the barn is full of bales. In a timber-trussed barn the box is first nailed, from the inside, front and back to the beam with 3in (7.5cm) nails to give a firm fixing. The front which has already had a 9in x 9in (23cm x 23cm) opening cut out of the corner, is then fixed to the open end with 1in (2.5cm) nails. Finally, the tray is nailed in front of the box.

In some cases, it may be necessary to support the platform on timber runners nailed to the underside of the box.

If the barn has steel roof trusses, it is best to nail vertical and horizontal pieces of timber to the box; these can be firmly roped, wired or G-cramped to the steelwork. Every ounce of ingenuity should be used when dealing with these barns, as very often they are the only suitable roosting and nesting-sites for miles around. Boxes can also be placed in corner sites and hung from ridge purlins, but virtually every barn demands its own solution. Barrels can be placed in disused lofts, but here access must be restricted while the birds are nesting.

Whether your boxes are occupied or not, keep the knowledge of their whereabouts restricted to as few as possible. Human predation is, unfortunately, a reality as is disturbance by well meaning but misguided birdwatchers. Never let any unwanted eyes see you checking a building and only visit occasionally, preferably towards dusk, so that if the adult is inadvertently flushed, it will quickly return.

A most important point is that the barn owl is included on Schedule 1 of the Bird Protection Act. This means that both the bird and its eggs are specially protected by law, and if you intend to visit your occupied nestboxes you must obtain a special Government Permit. If you see that the box is occupied early in the breeding season, it is probably best to watch from a safe distance, thus avoiding disturbing the birds and the need to become involved in such legalities. The Bird Protection Laws do not hinder the farmer from going about his normal business using the barn!

Eggs: 4-7 white. March to July. Incubation 32-34 days; fledging about 10 weeks. Frequently two broods.

GREAT TIT *Parus major*

Resident and generally distributed, scarcer in northern Scotland. Woodland, hedges, gardens.

Nests in tree or wall holes, or crevices. Also in second-hand nests, or the foundations of larger nests. If no natural sites are available, it may use letterboxes, flower pots, beehives and almost any kind of hole. Nest lined with a thick layer of hair or down.

Nestbox: enclosed, with 1⅛in (29mm) diameter entrance hole or slightly larger, interior depth at least 5in (12.5cm) from hole to floor, and floor at least 4in x 4in (10cm x 10cm). Great tits are the most enthusiastic customers for boxes, with blue tits coming second. They not uncommonly occupy the same box, the great tits taking over, covering the blue tits' eggs with a fresh lining and hatching only their own eggs (though mixed broods are not unknown). Tit boxes are successful even in woodland, where there is a shortage of old trees because management procedures do not tolerate them. Result is strong competition for sites.

Eggs: 5-11 white, splotched reddish brown. End April to June. Incubation 13-14 days; fledging about 3 weeks. One brood.

BLUE TIT *Parus caeruleus*

Resident and generally distributed except in north-west Scotland. Woodland, hedges, gardens.

Nests as great tit. Blue tits may go to a nestbox because the best natural sites have been taken by the dominant great tits.

Nestbox: enclosed, with 1in to 1⅜in (25mm to 30mm) entrance hole, otherwise as great tit.

Eggs: 7-14 (though there is a record of 19!), usually spotted light chestnut. Late April and May. Incubation 13-14 days; fledging 15-21 days. One brood. Blue tits breed most successfully in deciduous woodland, where there is an abundance of caterpillars. They breed less successfully in built-up areas, even though clutches are smaller to compensate for the poor food available.

Blue tit inside a nestbox, with nestlings

CHAPTER FIVE

Bird Table Watching

Now your birds have food, drink and a home, enjoy their company . . .

ONE OF the pleasures of bird table watching is the slow but steady way in which more and more species are being lured to join in. Not only kestrels and goshawks, but more and more of the birds that formerly kept us at some distance. Great spotted woodpeckers and long-tailed tits are much commoner visitors than they once were. Goldcrests, firecrests, cirl buntings, woodcock, common snipe, water rail, kingfishers and dipper — all these species have taken to the habit. Bearded tits have been encouraged to visit seed piles near reed beds at the Minsmere RSPB reserve. Little gulls have taken food scraps from a litter bin. It seems there is no limit to the possibilities. But whatever comes to visit, a well-found bird table will be a delight to watch, especially in winter. A continuous stream of finches and tits will share the pickings with starlings, sparrows and perhaps even woodpeckers and nuthatches.

Study the behaviour of your guests over a period of time. Birds are easily inclined to quarrel over their food, and these feeding squabbles are well observed at the bird table. One threatens another by posturing, gaping aggressively, spreading wings and tail. It is largely a game of bluff, since neither individual wants to come to blows, wasting energy and risking the loss of precious feathers, to say nothing of the danger from predators if they aren't keeping a proper watch. But the game has a serious object, because the winner gets the choicest titbit (and at other times the best perch, the best breeding territory and the most desirable mate). So the establishment of a pecking order is meaningful, and it plays a real part in everyday bird life.

The peck order or, more scientifically, dominance hierarchy, is so called because the experimental work which demonstrated

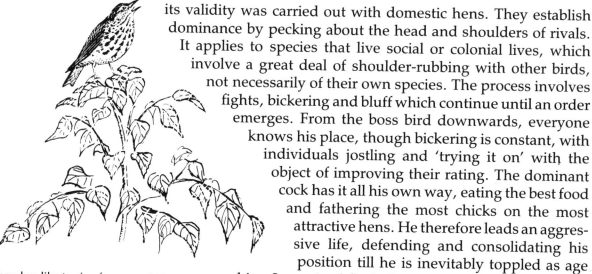

Thrushes like to sing from
a high perch

its validity was carried out with domestic hens. They establish dominance by pecking about the head and shoulders of rivals. It applies to species that live social or colonial lives, which involve a great deal of shoulder-rubbing with other birds, not necessarily of their own species. The process involves fights, bickering and bluff which continue until an order emerges. From the boss bird downwards, everyone knows his place, though bickering is constant, with individuals jostling and 'trying it on' with the object of improving their rating. The dominant cock has it all his own way, eating the best food and fathering the most chicks on the most attractive hens. He therefore leads an aggressive life, defending and consolidating his position till he is inevitably toppled as age creeps up on him. In a mixed flock there will still be a peck order, which explains why the starlings take precedence at the bird table, followed by house sparrows, great, blue, marsh or willow and coal tits in that order. In fact blue tits will rob great tits almost as often as they are robbed by them, with coal tits decidedly the weakest in the hierarchy.

Blackbirds fight amongst themselves, with a great deal of noisy chasing across the lawn and through the shrubbery. As a species they dominate song thrushes, taking earthworms from their beaks and waiting till they crack the meat out of snail shells before moving in to steal it. If you are lucky enough to have a resident mistle thrush, he will dominate both blackbird and song thrush. Starlings

Bird table fights involve
more bluff than blows;
birds cannot risk losing
too many feathers

The handsome magpie;
they build dome-shaped
nests in trees (*John
Hawkins/Eric & David
Hosking*)

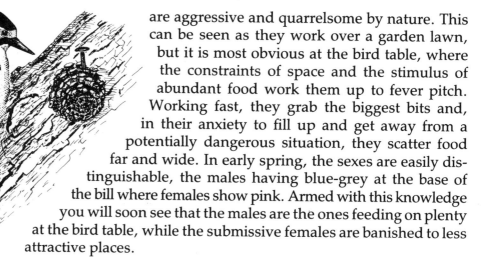

are aggressive and quarrelsome by nature. This can be seen as they work over a garden lawn, but it is most obvious at the bird table, where the constraints of space and the stimulus of abundant food work them up to fever pitch. Working fast, they grab the biggest bits and, in their anxiety to fill up and get away from a potentially dangerous situation, they scatter food far and wide. In early spring, the sexes are easily distinguishable, the males having blue-grey at the base of the bill where females show pink. Armed with this knowledge you will soon see that the males are the ones feeding on plenty at the bird table, while the submissive females are banished to less attractive places.

Great spotted woodpeckers come to gardens for fatty offerings like suet (or Pine Cone Surprise, p34)

Rarities

Great rarities have been spotted on bird tables. In the severe winter of 1954–5, while there was thick snow on the ground, an unfortunate American warbler, which had found itself in England after an unscheduled Atlantic crossing, showed up on a south Devon bird table. This myrtle warbler, the first record for Britain, established itself in vigorous ownership of the food supply, seeing off the resident blue tits.

Robins defend their territory with vigour

Starlings are sociable birds, but they are quick to take offence and quarrel

The first record of a red-throated thrush, *Turdus ruficolis*, to be seen in Britain was made in a north Buckinghamshire urban garden in the winter of 1978–9. A Siberian species, this one was looked at with a certain amount of suspicion since it seemed quite likely that it was an escaped cage bird. There are long-term trends to be discerned by studying the bird table. Great spotted woodpeckers and long-tailed tits appear to have come to stay, and the relatively recent colonisation of our islands by collared doves has been made easier by the freely available supply of food.

Not surprisingly, crows have learnt the advantages of Man-supplied food. Magpies, as part of a general increase in numbers, have become more common in country gardens as well as the

Starlings tend to take over a bird table

Predators

Raptors are well designed for their job as hunter-killers. Sparrowhawks have broad, rounded wings by comparison with the more open-country falcons like peregrines, which have been designed for speed. But sparrowhawks work in amongst the trees and hedgerows, and while they enjoy a fair turn of speed they are also able to engage in fast turns and complicated manoeuvres, a useful facility if you're chasing a wildly jinking small bird. Like the other birds of prey, they are able to turn their fourth toe so that it is pointing backwards, allowing a tight grip with two sharp-clawed toes on either side of the victim's body. And the forward component of the impact motion as they land on a victim causes the claws to lock automatically and grip fast, a sinister variation on the same mechanism that locks songbirds' feet to their roosting perch when they go to sleep. The bird must make a conscious effort to release its victim.

Sparrowhawks are not the only hunters which enjoy the living bounty of the bird table. Kestrels commonly take house sparrows and young starlings when they get the chance, behaviour that has been most observed in London, where they are now established as breeding birds. Voles are their preferred diet, and they find good hunting along railway embankments, but if small mammals are scarce they will take many birds, and a bird table will become more interesting to them.

Sparrowhawks may visit the bird table in search of
their dinner, but they are a natural hazard for small birds

opposite Sparrowhawks may take blue tits and chaffinches
from your garden, but they do not affect the long-term
numbers of small birds that visit you *(David Hosking)*

Blackbirds use the lawn
as an arena for their
territorial battles

suburbs. First they took the songbirds eggs and young, and then moved in to take the bird table food provided for them.

Jays will collect unshelled peanuts and carry them off for burying and subsequent digging up as a food store, in the same way that they bury vast numbers of acorns in autumn. This food storage is typical of other species such as nuthatches and tits, which hide food at a time when it is abundant, though it is particularly widespread amongst the crow family. It occurs when there is more food about than the birds are able to eat, and quite apart from obviously suitable items like nuts, they will hide bread or cheese. This family propensity to store food gave rise to the 'thieving magpie' legend. And while wild birds do not carry off gold rings and diamond necklaces, it is likely that tame ones might do so when they are deprived of their natural foraging.

Migration studies and ringing

The seasonal movements of birds have always fascinated us, and we have long sought to unravel their mystery. In part, there is an element of sport in the pursuit, an enjoyment of the challenges offered in trapping and marking the birds. There is, however, a more serious purpose, that of discovering more about birds' lifestyles and popu-

Jays collect large numbers
of acorns in autumn

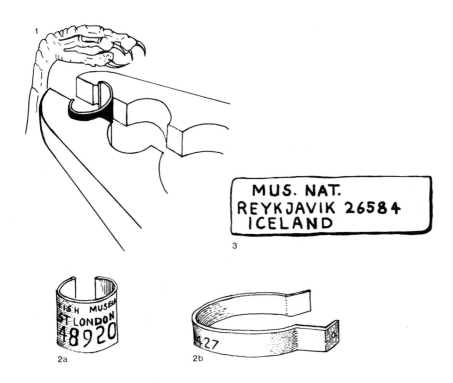

1 Special pliers used to fit rings to bird legs
2a Butt rings are used on most British birds, but some of the larger species need to be fitted with a clip (2b)
3 Many countries have their own ringing schemes

MUS. NAT.
REYKJAVIK 26584
ICELAND

Bills

If you take a close look at garden birds you will often find that some of them display abnormalities of the beak, and starlings seem particularly prone. It is not uncommon to see a bird with a down-curved bill as much as a couple of inches long, curlew-like. Such birds seem to manage well enough, although sometimes this must be because they are paid special attention at bird tables, for they find it very difficult to pick up natural food. A bird's bill of course, acts as its hand. The horny sheath is a projection of the jaws, and like a finger-nail it is growing all the time. Normally wear and tear compensate for the rate of growth and the bill remains at a useful operating length; a tool used in nest building, preening and feeding. If damaged, the bill will regenerate, but the process takes time, and the bird must be at a disadvantage meanwhile. Oddly shaped bills are not always caused by an accident; they can result from a genetic abnormality. On the whole it is surprising how little annoyance they seem to cause — though we just don't see the worst-afflicted birds because they don't survive.

Jays bury acorns when they are plentiful, then dig them up in winter when food is hard to come by *(John Hawkins/ Eric & David Hosking)*

Song thrushes hunt snails when other food is not easily available; they break them open on carefully-chosen 'anvils', in this case a bottle but more usually a stone *(Brian Hawkes)*

lation dynamics, information which can be of great value in assessing the ecological effects of changes in land use, for instance.

Many and various are the nuggets of information gathered as a result of long-term bird ringing. We know that some birds live long lives, though the average expectancy is very short indeed, especially in the case of songbirds. But an oystercatcher may live thirty-four years, a herring gull thirty-two. The oldest recorded swallow covered nearly a quarter of a million miles (over 200,000km) during its sixteen years of life, an Arctic tern half a million (over 400,000km) in its twenty-seven years. The oldest swift, at sixteen, must have flown over four million miles in its lifetime. In cold weather during the winter of 1963, searching for new feeding grounds, a redwing covered 2,400 miles (about 3,860km) in three days. A swift born and bred in Oxford, was recovered in Madrid three days after it left the nest. We know that small birds increase their weight just before migration. A sedge warbler which weighs about ⅓oz (10g) normally, will build up to more than ⅔oz (20g) thus carrying enough fat to fuel a non-stop flight of 2,000 miles (about 3,200km). They complete this distance in

Large numbers of birds —
starlings in this case —
take advantage of the
roosting facilities on oil
rigs at migration time

Sedge warblers may double their weight in a few days before a migration journey which will use up their 'fuel' and reduce them to normal

just three days, crossing Europe, the Mediterranean and North Africa, possibly even overflying the Sahara to reach Senegal or Ghana, having slimmed down to half take-off weight, a return to normal.

Chris Perrins trapped blue tits at a well-stocked bird table and found that it was visited by more than a hundred different individuals in the course of the morning, while many of us had assumed that our bird table was feeding just a few locals.

Leisure time involvement

The best way to learn about birds and to meet other people who enjoy them is to join the Young Ornithologists Club (address page 92), or, if you are past that stage, the Royal Society for the Protection of Birds (page 93).

What are the opportunities for working voluntarily with birds? After joining the YOC or the RSPB, probably the best way to get involved in your local area is to join the local Naturalists' Trust or Bird Society. Through them your leisure time hobby can be harnessed for valuable and exciting research.

The British Trust for Ornithology is the major organisation which initiates and co-ordinates research which involves the efforts of a

Swallows congregate in flocks before their long migration journey to South Africa

network of birdwatchers covering the whole of Britain. If you want to become actively concerned with census or ringing work, then you need to become a member. The standards are high, the BTO operates to serious scientific standards, but the range of work is wide enough to encompass everyone from the conscientious beginner to the dedicated professional. The work tends to consist of some form of census — statistical recording of numbers breeding, passing by and wintering — or ringing. And there is no doubt that this work is invaluable. For birds, and bird numbers, are among the most sensitive indicators of the health of our environment. Keeping an eye on changes in their numbers provides essential information for those who make wildlife laws.

Herons have been counted at their breeding heronries every year since 1928; the total number in the British Isles is somewhere around 10,000 pairs

'Abandoned' fledglings

A grating and insistent chirping from the back of the flower border is an easy give-away to the presence of a newly fledged song thrush crouching fat-bellied, stump-tailed and guileless on the ground among the plants at the base of the hedge. Brothers and sisters are doubtless close by but with luck they are sensibly perched in the depths of the thick prickly hedge where they will be a little safer than the wide-eyed innocent sitting on the ground. For the first day or two after they have left the nest the fledglings ability to fly will be rudimentary; they may be quite good at flying downwards but pretty hopeless going back up. During this time they are in the most vulnerable period of their lives, unable to defend themselves, unequipped for escape and soft targets for a garden predator. This is the time of year above all others to keep the cat indoors during the daytime!

The parent birds will continue to feed the youngsters when they are out of the nest for a week or two (double-brooded pairs may even have to feed two consecutive broods of young at the same time) and during the early days of the period after they leave the nest the youngsters readily give the impression of being lost and forsaken. But they are not really abandoned, so harden your heart a little and resist the obvious temptation to take them in and look after them yourself. Watch carefully and you will see that the parents do know where they are and are bringing food to them regularly. It may indeed be a dangerous and vulnerable time for these hopefuls but it is a gauntlet they have to run and we should leave them to take their chance, knowing that the parents will bring them the food they need. It is a much better option than taking their fate into our own hands.

A Career with Birds

A CAREER with birds can encompass an astonishing range of professions and activities, some academic, some manual, some more obvious than others. A good degree in zoology can lead to research into any aspect of bird life — behaviour, breeding, migration, food requirements or the effects of the weather for example. These things matter to us, as people, because birds are part of our economy. They eat and transport seeds, aid or damage crops, control undesirable insects, cause aircraft accidents by 'bird strike' and provide food for the table. So, one way or another, they make jobs available for scientists in the fields of forestry, medicine, agriculture, fisheries, game conservation, and so on. The top-flight scientists need assistants, laboratory workers and other helpers, skilled and unskilled, academic or manual. A most useful guide and starting point for the kind of job opportunities there are available and the qualifications required for them is the booklet *Careers in Biology*, published by the Institute of Biology (see address on page 93).

Biological work is sometimes pure research — pushing back the frontiers of our knowledge about a bird's life — and sometimes it is mainly for economic reasons, as with pest control or more effective agriculture. Either way, you cannot study birds in isolation — they need to be seen in the context of their habitat. Habitat control and management is one of the most exciting and rewarding aspects of nature conservation, affecting the lives and fortunes of all creatures and plants of the community. This is the work of estates and reserve management, and town and country planning, for example, and involves people from many fields: geologists and water engineers, hedgers and ditchers, biologists and farmers, foresters, cartographers, and so on. Taken to extremes, at the RSPB's famous

Reed warbler

reserve at Minsmere, in East Anglia, the low-lying coastal land is managed solely for the benefit of birds. There the skills of those who design and operate the sluices, shift the very soil to make the 'scrapes' and islands, and plan the planting and maintenance of the vegetation are all brought into play. Although some people argue that it is unhealthy to create reserves specifically set aside from normal everyday activities, such reserves and sanctuaries are probably vital in an increasingly agricultural and industrial country like ours.

Management of this kind is carried out by the RSPB, and other organisations, such as the Nature Conservancy Council, The National Trust, The Game Conservancy Council and local Naturalists' Trusts. Such work influences the comings and goings of wild birds, sick and injured birds, and even dead ones. Taxidermy, the work of stuffing the dead skin of an animal, requires an intimate knowledge of the way of life of the subject — how a bird stands, moves or flies — if the final product is faithfully to portray the living version. So, although the taxidermist may deal with corpses, he must study their living relatives in the field.

Captive birds, usually exotic, form a well known part of zoos and bird collections throughout the country. The inmates must be fed and cleaned, and in some cases serious research and breeding programmes are under way, in an attempt to reinforce natural populations in the wild. Sometimes wild birds become captive for a while, as a result of sickness or injury. Birds may be brought in by cats or knocked by passing cars, and although shocked and exhausted they are often uninjured and require nothing more than a period of peace and quiet in a warm, dark cardboard box to restore them to normal. But broken wings, broken legs or damage from oil pollution, for example, all common misfortunes, need active treatment. Such birds should be taken to a vet or to the RSPCA, or to a reputable bird hospital — many of which are run privately by people who devote their time to treating such casualties. Your nearest RSPCA branch may be able to help with addresses of such organisations. It is a difficult and time consuming business treating, feeding, housing and rehabilitating birds which have been damaged, or have left the nest prematurely, or been orphaned. And people who undertake such work need total dedication and considerable financial resources. Not a job to be undertaken lightly, or without proper professional guidance.

To work in direct contact with birds — as a reserve warden, at a bird observatory or at a wildfowl collection — has a tremendous attraction which can be judged by the enormous numbers of applicants for the relatively few jobs available. There are many more opportunities connected with teaching and communicating an interest in, and enthusiasm for, birds, which are just as important as a concern for their welfare. Apart from formal teaching in school — at all levels — we learn about birds through radio and television, books and magazine articles, and museum exhibitions. Such productions all need their teams of workers, from cameramen and photographers to writers and designers, artists, taxidermists and so on. All must study their birds, if they are to be successful.

By communicating an enthusiasm for birds and imparting an understanding of their value and importance to the planet, teachers are laying up treasure for the birds of the future. The RSPB, first formed in 1889 and now with a strength of well over half a million members and managing 116 reserves, must take a place of honour among the many organisations which work on behalf of wildlife. The RSPB has research scientists, film makers, wardens, and other specialists — full-time staff earning their living with birds.

left
In Florida, ospreys take freely to artificial nest sites; perhaps they will soon learn to do this in Scotland *(Tony Soper)*

far left
The hen chaffinch incubates her eggs for about twelve days, then both parents will feed the young on insects; most of the year they feed on seeds and they will come to bird tables for peanuts (Roger Wilmshurst/FLPA)

below
RSPB wardens on Speyside create nest sites by some clever work with chain saws; everyone hopes these nest holes will attract the rare crested tits *(Tony Soper)*

Useful Addresses

The Young Ornithologists' Club, The Lodge, Sandy, Bedfordshire, SG19 2DL

In 1965 the Royal Society for the Protection of Birds set up a special club for young people — like you — interested in birdwatching and wildlife protection. The club is known as the Young Ornithologists' Club or YOC for short (an ornithologist is anyone who is interested in birds and enjoys observing them in their natural surroundings). Today, this club has a membership of more than 90,000 and is the largest club of its kind in the world.

Bird Life:
The club's magazine, *Bird Life*, is posted directly to members six times a year. *Bird Life* is brilliant! It is packed with full colour photographs and fascinating articles on a wide variety of topics. There are contributions from famous wildlife enthusiasts, artists, photographers and members alike. I am sure you will want to contribute to *Bird Life*. There are now even more pages of amazing and mysterious facts about our birds and other wildlife, as well as plenty of information telling you what's going on and where.

Super prizes:
Each year there are dozens of exciting quizzes (some easy, others more difficult) as well as challenging competitions. You can test your skills in photography, writing, painting and even your imagination. Prizes include, amongst other things, cameras, books, posters and binoculars! You will also be able to enter for the YOC's national 'Young Ornithologist of the Year' award — the highest honour for young birdwatchers.

Bird protection:
YOC members can help with special surveys and projects. By taking part *you* could be providing the RSPB's Research Department with the valuable answers to its questions, and the information it needs to help save our wild birds.

Fun, excitement and adventure:
The YOC offers you so many opportunities to meet new friends with similar interests. With over 270 YOC Groups throughout Britain and Northern Ireland you have the chance to join in with local activities. There are film shows, quiz evenings, fun-days and much more! Holiday courses and Members' Days are arranged — our experts are waiting to take *you* on these nature adventure trips. You could end up spending a week on Fair Isle, or perhaps a weekend at Sheringham (do you know where these exciting places are?).

Nature reserves:
As a YOC member you will be able to visit FREE more than 100 RSPB reserves where there are special birds to be seen — the ones *you* have helped to save — plus many other exciting animals and plants.

Free Bumper Bird Pack . . .
On joining, you will receive the YOC's exclusive 'Bumper Bird Pack', containing a first bonus copy of *Bird Life* free; a wallchart; a booklet full of birdwatching tips; official YOC membership card and armbadge; heaps more information, and all the details of how to get the most out of the YOC inside our new 'Barn Owl' presentation pack!

This is your chance to discover the exciting and colourful world of birds and other wildlife — a world that starts on your very own doorstep.

Write to Peter Holden. The YOC National Organiser, and ask for details.

The Royal Society for the Protection of Birds — same address as YOC. Write for sales catalogue and membership details.

The British Trust for Ornithology, Beech Grove, Tring, HP23 5NR. Write for list of publications and membership details.

The address of your nearest Bird Club will be at the Public Library.

Institute of Biology, 41 Queen's Gate, London, SW7 5HU. Write for a copy of *Careers in Biology*.

SUPPLIERS OF BIRD FOODS (Please don't buy peanuts from other suppliers unless they are *guaranteed* aflatoxin-free).

C.J. Wildbird Foods, The Rea, Upton Magna, Shrewsbury, SY4 4UB. Top quality peanuts and bird seed.

John E. Haith Ltd, Park St, Cleethorpes, South Humberside, DN35 7NF. Seeds and soft bill foods.

Trill wild bird food is the best seed-mix for finches and many song birds. From supermarkets and garden stores.

Further Reading

Here are some ideas for books which you might find useful.

Best single-volume bird book . . .
The Popular Handbook of Rarer British Birds, P. Hollom (Witherby)

Big bumper books . . .
The Complete Book of British Birds (AA/RSPB)
Birds of the World, Oliver Austin (Hamlyn)
The World of Birds, James Fisher (Macdonald)

Introductions to birdwatching . . .
Birdwatching (Usborne Publishing)
Discover Birds, Ian Wallace (Deutsch)
Birds, Christopher Perrins (Collins)
Watching Birds, Ian Wallace (Usborne Pocket Naturalist)

For places to go . . .
Where to Go Birdwatching (RSPB nature reserves) (BBC Books)
The New Where to Watch Birds, J. Gooders (Deutsch)

For identification . . .
The Country Life Guide to Birds of Britain and Europe, B. Bruun (Country Life)
The Birds of Britain and Europe, H. Heinzel (Collins)

A Field Guide to the Birds of Britain and Europe, R. Peterson (Collins)

For more details of nestboxes and bird gardening . . .
The Garden Bird Book, David Glue (Macmillan)
The Bird Table Book, T. Soper (David & Charles)

For a month-by-month account of bird gardening . . .

Birds in Your Garden, T. Soper & R. Lovegrove (Webb & Bower)

You can get them from the Public Library, but some of them are so worthwhile you will want to have your own copy.

TEACHERS' GUIDES
The RSPB publishes a series of useful guides which provide background information and suggest avenues of bird study for exploration. Titles include subjects like 'Bird studies using school grounds', 'Birds and mathematics', 'Bird movements and migration'. Write to the Education Dept, RSPB, The Lodge, Sandy, Beds, SG19 2DL for further information.

Young Ornithologists' Club outings visit famous reserves and the best birdwatching places; sometimes they meet famous people like David Bellamy *(Roger Tidman/ FLPA)*

The RSPB bus travels the country — don't miss a chance to see inside *(Roger Tidman/FLPA)*

Index

Photographs and drawings are indicated by *italic* type

Aflatoxin, 14, 29

Bath, bird, *36*
Bills, 28, 81
Bird baths, 35
Binoculars, 6-12
Biology, Institute of, 87, 93
Birdfood Standards Assoc., 29
Birdsong tapes, 13
Bird tables, 24, *26*
Blackbird, *11*, 28, *29*, *38*, 44, 48, 63, 65, 74, *80*
Blackcap, 32
Brambling, 32
British Birds magazine, 6, 49
British Trust for Ornithology, 55, 84, 93
Bunting, cirl, 73

Careers, 87
Chaffinch, *7*, 32, *38*, *90*
Chiffchaff, 32
C. J. Wildbird Foods, 93
Crow, 77

Dipper, 73
Dominance hierarchy, 73
Dove, collared, 77
Dovecote, *54*, *55*
Dunnock, 31

Eggs, 53
Evergreens, 21

Feathers, 44
Field Guides, 13
Finches, 28
Firecrest, 73
Fledglings, 'abandoned', 86
Flycatcher, pied, *56*
Flycatcher, spotted, *48*, 65, *65*, *66*, *67*
Focussing, 9
Forestry Commission, 32

Game Conservancy Council, 88
Goldcrest, 32, 73
Goldfinch, 16, *17*
Goshawk, 73

Greenfinch, 31
Gull, herring, 83

Heron, 33, *85*
Hoopoe, *20*

Ivy, 21, *21*

Jay, 32, 80, *80*, *82*

Kestrel, 64, 73, 79
Kingfisher, 32, 73

Magpie, *42*, *56*, *75*, 77
Mallard, 61
Martin, house, 53, 57, 58, *59*
Material, nest, 53
Migration, 80ff
Minsmere, 73, 88
Moorhen, *67*

National Trust, 88
Nature Conservancy Council, 88
Nerine Nurseries, 59
Nestboxes, 48ff
Nesting, 47
Nettles, 16
Nuthatch, 73

Osprey, *90*
Owl, barn, 68
Oystercatcher, 83

Peanuts, 29
Pecking order, 73
Perrins, Chris, 84
Plants, pond, 41
Ponds, 36, *37*

Rail, water, 73
Raptors, 79
Recipes, 34
Robin, *10*, 28, 31, 44, 52, 61, *61*, 63, 76
Royal Society for the Protection of Birds, 12, 25, 26, 32, 84, 93

Siskin, *18*, 32, *32*
Snipe, 73
Sparrowhawk, *78*, 79, *79*
Sparrow, house, *40*, 59
Sparrow, tree, *58*
Spruce, 22
Starling, 23, *42*, 62, 73, 77, 83
Starwort, water, *41*
Suet, 32
Swallow, 16, *85*
Swift, *52*, 83

Teal, *45*
Tern, arctic, 83
Thrushes, 28
Thrush, red-throated, 77
Thrush, song, *20*, *29*, *46*, *82*
Tit, bearded, 73
Tit, blue, *18*, 43, 52, *70*, *72*, *72*, 84
Tit, coal, *33*
Tit, great, *7*, *14*, *33*, *71*, 72

Tit, long-tailed, 77
Topography, bird, 8
Treecreeper, *21*, 22, *32*, *50*
Trees, 21
Trill wild bird food, 29, 33, 93

Wagtail, pied, *24*
Warbler, myrtle, 76
Warbler, reed, *88*
Warbler, sedge, 83, *84*
Water, 35ff
Weeds, 14
Wellingtonia, 22
Winter feeding, 23
Woodcock, 73
Woodpeckers, 32
Woodpecker, great spotted, *30*, 73, 76, 77
Wren, 28, *57*

Young Ornithologists' Club, 84, 92

Zoos, 88